Musings of a Young Man

Christian Fowler

Copyright © 2019 Christian Fowler

ISBN: 9781079986884

The truth you know is not for words,
for words will only go so far
They carry truth like little birds,
but there aren't words for what you are

You long to speak of what you feel,
but eloquence is of distraction
I ask that you find feeling real,
and learn that truth is said in action

Part 2: Musings

Dedication

Dedicated to my mother, Toni, who cultivated my wonder and desire for depth. To my father, David, who cultivated my heart and relationship with Father God. To my precious friends and siblings who conversed with me and drew me out. To my dear friend Anaiah, who continues to draw out depth and spirit. To my Lord alive, and ancestors passed, who have served integral roles in my development.

Forward

Christian Fowler has always had a very unique way of looking at life, seeing it as more of a mystery to dive into than a progression or linear journey. He has always been fascinated in the things of life that most people do not know much about, and has therefore taken a very different path than anyone I have ever known. As his older brother, I watched him first delve into many eccentric fields of study, from magic/illusion to astronomy, from ancient history to eschatology. He was always on his own track, but it was not until he found books like "The Cepher" and "Meditations" by Marcus Aurelius that I began to see the depth of his wisdom coming into his every conversation.

He would often make a suggestion as if it were the other person's idea, one that would leave them so perplexed by his depth of understanding that it was clear to all who witnessed that the idea was not one's but Christian's. But the idea would then lead all who listened into a deeper understanding of the topic than ever before.

Similarly, this composition of his musings, discoveries and the truth that he has found through divine revelation and communion with The Spirit will lead its readers into a deeper understanding of each topic discussed in this book. It is not a book to read through too quickly, for the true value will be found in the slow ingestion of each sentence, and one may take longer to read through it than the size would suggest. I would suggest with each encounter you have with his poetry, to try to take an extra moment and grasp the depth in his words.

If there is something that bothers you to read, or that you disagree with, set it aside and return to it later. If your spirit agrees with it the second time, you may discover the truth as he has, or you may choose to disagree. You will not find sources for all that he writes, because much the truth within him comes from within him. As the same spirit that held residence in C.S. Lewis, Paul the Apostle, or even Christ Jesus, resides in Christian, and resides within you. And it is through this connection with the Infinite Truth that truth comes into this world. So sit back and enjoy, or dive headfirst into the mysteries, musings and multitude of truths of The Spirit, delivered to you by Christian Fowler in Musings of a Young Man

-Daniel Michael Fowler

Part 1:

Poetry

Chapter I
Sand & Cities

The Swarm

The beauty of our tribe fell upon my
father's eyes
The dusk was filled with music while the
sun was in the skies
Timbrels shook in unison, the women
danced in lines
Then night began to fall, as the winds
began to rise

The wind flew through my hair, sand ran
upon the ground
Dunes resembled flutes, playing tunes of
joyful sound
Laughter reached the stars, a moon could
now be found,
When suddenly, breezes turned to swarms
of plagues around

In an instant, all men rose, the
clicking growing close
Locusts embrace drought, and the water
when it flows,
they care not when it's cold, nor either
when it's warm,
but locusts tend to run when the sands
begins to storm

Our women took to tents, our babes began
to fuss,
It took a simple look to know the
plagues were not for us

No interest in our food, so we didn't
feel the swarm,
we prayed it be the same as the sands
began to storm

It covered up and smothered us, until it
blew away,
then came again and stayed until it went
upon its way
"Desert storms are desert norms", Father
often said,
as quickly as it came, it went, none of
us left dead

"We desert tribes never die, and that we
owe to God,
no clearer sky you'll ever find, nor any
land so broad
Keep in praise, be quick to raise, and
slow to judgement form,
no doubt you will be safe, my son, when
sands begin to storm"

Cairo

In my memory, it's there, it's the sand
within my hair
It's the wind within the sails, the
cliff at which I stared
At first, I wasn't home, for I left that
place to roam
I left you once, my love, for reasons
only known by poem

Not yet knowing of your worth, I left
that place to learn
I left the walls and domes, as the tomes
let oil burn
I toiled in concern, for in other things
I yearned
But for what I thought was great, I
strayed, never to return

But I began to miss the scrolls, to miss
how Aramaic rolls
Greek influence weakened, with Egyptians
growing old
I'd fell for Greece's springs, felt the
wind of Egypt's wings,
but love had pierced me more than the
sand of desert sting

For I knew my line of sires, and I knew
from whom I sprang
But the parents who begot me were not
from the place I came
I was descendant line of Abram, in

```
         Ishmael's domain
I stood out, but truly knew the people's
         love was all the same

Except for her, my toil, my blood boiled
            when it dawned,
  that for her I did yearn more than for
          the words of the Quran
Knowing it may be too late, fate set me
              on the sea,
   and from Cairo I set sail, to finally
          hold my wife to be
```

Sands of Time

My bath was drawn with water from a fire
and a spring
The harp that played beside me filled
the water with its string
The bubbling surface broke when I arose
to issue leave,
to the harpist and the melody she'd
effortlessly sing

I stood and grasped a towel, desert wind
entered my lungs
The nighttime breath of cold had only
barely just begun
Gardens round the palace had their day
under the sun,
and the camels all exhaled after their
journey with someone

Gold slid up my arms, a purple sash
adorned my waist
The tower sounded trumpets and the
guards opened the gates
Festivities begun when the moon replaced
the sun,
the chefs prepared the meal, and the
halls began to drum

The wind that night was magic, as with
every night before
The candlelight not static, as the
sandstone in the floor
Silk adorned the dress of every

princess, well adored,
and the apples found their way into the
mouth of every boar

The room below my own was the first to
play a chord,
the courtyard of the kingdom, where the
servants greet the lords
Kings, and guards alike, retired all
their Saracen swords,
and camels took to eat, where some water
they were poured

On any night but this, in my palace of a
home,
I'd sit upon the roof, see the sky, and
dream of Rome
I'd look at out the desert, touched by
breath of God, alone
Conversing with a servant, all of which
I'd always known

But rewind the sands of time, two
allotments of a week,
invited, by my father, were the kings of
which I speak
For engagement of his eldest, an
occasion with a feast,
and right outside my door was the
roaring Middle East

My fingers entered rings, and a diamond
found my ear,
My shirt beset my shoulders, as the
crowds began to cheer

Something trifle I should mention, or it
      be taken as a crime,
 is that I am my father's eldest, now
    resume the sands of time

Parables

I haven't been home in longer than life,
and still sob at the thought of leaving
my wife
So I'll make my way home, and when I
arrive,
will the home that I know be the place
that I find?

It's been a long time, but it's waiting
for me
The way which things were is the way
which they'll be
The temples still glowing, the gardens
still growing,
the home I remember is the home that
I'll see

Will the sun in his kiln still be
setting gold?
Or parables plenty from the mouths of
old?
Will my balcony lie beneath Jordan's
wealth?
And my father still bold in his former
health?

Will the roof of my room be my hiding
place?
Will the stars again share all their
hidden ways?
Will the days still sting, will
sandstone sing,

is the language I spoke still the one
that I speak?

Will my city be the same or will it be a
ruin?
if it's crumbled is it covered by the
sand that blew in?
Did the God that was there crumble with
the rest?
Or is the Lord of that world all that's
really left

Do I remember it all just to know He's
here?
That He was, and He is, and I shouldn't
fear?
For he was in people, my land and my
heart
and they may have decayed, but He's
never far

Arabian Nights

It was the clearest of all those Arabian
nights
She chose a tall wall and we scaled its
heights
The dirt below us known by a day of
life,
and the door posts shown by their
dimming lights

The stars we used to look at were twice
as bright,
than any seen now on the darkest nights
We sat on our wall with our sight on it
all,
backs to the palace and the sky in our
eyes

I laughed harder that night than I
thought I could
And I told more to that girl than I
thought I would
From below, the echoes of strings filled
our ears,
and our fears took a plunge from the
place we stood

The counter part to my heart, and my
equal in zeal,
as our outer-world notions were equally
real
We'd read of the scrolls that have since
been concealed

that my sire had authored, words by
Yahweh revealed

Enochian blood gave lift to Ishmael's
heel,
the first day that Yahweh saw it ideal,
to kindle a friendship that's still in
the heart,
of with whom it started, in whom it is
sealed

She'd hear of my knowledge, both inside
and out
Only she knew the secrets that came from
my mouth
Two thousand B.C., yet I said the same
things
Only, then, with a friend who'd also
seen wings

She used to sing me to sleep, so
immensely deep
In exchange, what I wrote, she'd always
have me read
Our place atop the wall was ever so
tall,
but it was worth it every time for the
things we'd see

I'd known her for years, but haven't
seen her in ages
I've scoured the crowds, and thousands
of pages
Before falling asleep, sometimes I'll
read and I'll sing

Too long ago I never woke from her
melody

The girl I remember, she could see like
I see
She saw Him in awe and she sought
mystery
And sometimes still, in clear Arabian
skies,
I'll see there's still more to this
story

Chapter II
Fire & Iron

Shackles

The metal that binds is not natural, nor
right
It's a restrictive attachment that may
fall in His light
For one, not another, yet chains for us
all
And the key He presents, only few can
recall

All instruction He gave, they forget it
being taught
Those one's have lost sight, and for
them it seems not,
near foot, nor hand, and yet they
demand,
the key to their shackles, be produced
from a thought

Free will is our own, and some abuse its
choice
They're still much restricted, chains,
key, and their voice
But for reason or another, they choose
to keep close,
the chains that make them different, all
links self imposed

And then there are few, who attempt to
open locks,
with the wrong key, the wrong force,
like a boat without a dock
Some talk and they walk like their free

from their strains
But honest to God, we all still have
chains

And God has the reigns, to loosen or
wrong
The chains that are present are there
till they're gone
For reason or another, some don't
disappear
These shackles are guilt, our faults and
our fears

The key can be given to those who stand
true,
to what they've been taught, but these
people are few
But thank God for His mercy, upon me and
on you
These chains can be formed, and
shattered, too

Fire Comes and Fire Fades

Fire comes, and fire fades
But heat remains where wounds hold pain
what then, my friend, do we gain,
if scars are gone, but hurt remains?

When time presents an open wound,
just know that hope will never move
It's in the breeze that does reveal,
that in Jehovah, all is healed

Sealed in the smiles that you see,
is Christ above, Lord of thee
And for all you've ever learned to
trust,
God will polish the rusted piece

The piece of work, the piece of art
He'll bring to light, all you are
And there in peace our God will guard,
the one he's cherished from the start

Fire comes, and fire fades
And it's okay, if on those days,
we fall down and lose our way
Far better now than left at bay

The plan of our Father is never wrong
His strength and arm reach near and far
For faith in Christ won't leave you lost
And in that way, give hope to God

23

Don't Yawn

I want fire and ice in these eyes of
mine
I want God's light to burn inside
Relentless, constant, tested, tried
I give my submission to be His pride

I give my heart as a part of His Bride
I desire His fire in my path, He'll
guide
I pray my story, in His glory, He'll
hide
To Him is my strength, for by Him, I
abide

I've tried, I've lied, I've smiled and
cried
I've wept in the mercy of His Son, who
died
I stride like I'm tall, but it's Him, I
recall,
that gave angels wings to fly

"Ride strong, ride on, buck up, don't
yawn"
"Emotion breaks men, because steel's
bred in brawn"
"Don't question the system, or you'll
fail to move on"
I think we need more sons, we've got
enough pawns

From dusk till dawn, chisel and break me

We have enough boys who can shave, so
remake me
Muscles must burn, before there is gain
So my spiritual growth is worth physical
pain

Through rain and through storm, God
raises up men
Causes Sons to form in their repentance
for sin
Let me be no different, a Son now than
from them
Let me bear the weight of good fruit as
a stem

And as a gem that is rustic, but you
have the tools,
to remove all this rust and, if it's you
that approves,
then I'll walk on, careful, looking
ahead
Focused my sight into where God has led

And so, Father, I pray, you shatter the
base,
of the boys in this naive, crumbling
race
Of humans, women, children, the like
That you raise up Sons, and set men in
their place

Chapter III
Heavens & Earth

Foretold

I was looking at stars while standing in
the cold
I took two breaths and my chest then
froze
The moon pulled tide as its surface
broke,
and the Earth then stopped as its roll
plateaued

The cathedral steeples toppled in shock,
as Sydney's harbors sunk their docks
Rome's arena and Greece' Athena,
crumbled and broke as the sun couldn't
walk

Artist expressed their minds, or tried
as inspiration left poets and wells went
dry
Prophets woke to their visions dim,
as this world itself churned within

Books taught nothing as wisdom fled
The ocean's hue turned crimson red
The moon then bled from blasphemy,
and words past cursed then met the sea

As stars dug craters in nature's side,
young men loosened their grip on pride
Gold shattered dust as the wind picked
up
But God declared that it wasn't enough

So he sent then angels to unroll scrolls
As mountains like maps, were flipped in
folds
He told of this day, when the martyrs of
bold,
begged for justice, in the end foretold

So God then whispered and Earth howled
back
For the words of The Lord keep the world
intact
In fact, you could say, these days of
death,
ushered to Earth, the Father's breath

The Great Deluge

The clouds grew thick horizon lines,
this Earth bore far too many signs
Wells to gush and winds to rush,
rains to flush out hidden mines

Mines to find our covered gold,
mined, not sold, to men of old
Those men, renowned, soon to drown,
bound to see what prophets told

Watchers in their height observed,
God knows we got all we deserved
Those heathen breed hurt human seed,
and found their share of hurt reserved

In thought to keep our best alive,
Yahweh saw to keep some five,
that in refuge from great deluge,
he'd set afloat few men and wives

He gave way, that they'd embark,
and day by day, they'd built an ark
But fear of nothing gripped our gil,
for we could not discern His will

No creature heeded Noah's plea,
Not one on Earth, not even me
For in our pride, we took to die,
and perished under vengeful seas

Doves & Ravens

They say doves and ravens fly the same,
yet different birds with different names
Though one's revered, and one is feared,
I've seen tears chase doves away

I've heard some wild black birds sing,
not caw, but call sweet black bird
things
and I've seen doves that blaspheme love
And felt enough to know it stings

But I've known doves to rest on Jesus
And seen enough, to know He sees us
And I know ravens fed the prophet,
that God works in His ravens often

Though one is gentle, and one is harsh,
I've seen that feathers don't make
hearts,
For gentle doves build iron havens,
and love shines in the darkest ravens

I've heard that birds can't see their
wings,
or hear the pretty things they sing
Still different birds with different
names
though doves and ravens fly the same

30

gods

Before the first man had been there,
before knowledge was known of a path,
before records had writ of Him in man,
or first vessels of light and clay
cracked

Before the soul wore of a torn gown,
before the spirit of Him was in a man,
no account could be drawn upon by them,
and consequence had not began

But still what was written within Him,
endowed by who now was within,
was law and was laden before Him,
was light upon light before sin

Though soul was of God far before then,
long before it had inhabited flesh
his carnal knew naught of it's origin,
and had to recall power afresh

Guided by subtleties, peace and a light,
that one set a new precedent now,
though led astray, he remembered his way
and was the first to return to the light

Then millions on billions followed
along,
through their memory, learned of it all
they on their way, up into space,
to the greatness of their unique call

And now it's on us, to recall who we
are,
to remember from whence we came,
to love and to grow, venture to know,
and ascend on and up to the same

And as it all passes, becoming a sphere,
few worlds of the sun will sink back,
and we'll become gods, leading them on,
just like they were the gods of our past

Chapter IV
Rain & Waves

Far Off

Far off in the distance,
where wind blows off the sea,
and the sun has long been set,
she finds a place to breathe

Far beyond the lights,
where night reigns in a breeze,
the moon sleeps on the waters,
bright enough to see the trees

Far off by the blue,
she walked without her shoes
all to hear her Lord,
His tide in ocean tunes

Far out within the ocean,
creatures sleep in crowds
fins depart from motion,
the sky tucked in its clouds

Far out as ocean deep,
with her toes in island sand,
all but her was fast asleep,
and she blessed Hawaiian land

She herself found peace,
as she thought of all far off
for this had been her dream,
as she'd never left her loft

Island Storm

Not too long ago, there was a storm on
my island
Fast asleep in my home, between the sea
and the highland,
I was a sway in my hammock, til' the
rain met my clothes,
so I stayed, got soaked, then I laughed
and I rose

I sealed the screen door, and I walked
down the hall,
to see grey shadows dance on my blue
kitchen walls
Not trying to stall, I sanded off
unaware,
that I've honestly always had sand in my
hair

So I threw on my flops, and I hopped in
my Jeep,
I said a prayer to God that my island
He'd keep
Though storms were the norm, no one
wished them away,
our blessed ancestors taught us always
to pray

So I drove down the mud soaked road to
my home
When thunderclaps flashed me back to a
time I would roam
I don't know what happened, but I was

suddenly warm,
as it occurred to me that I was in my
first island storm

The water a whirl with blue eyed boys
with blond curls,
and orange fiery light in the eyes of
island girls
My brother, a drummer, would sing beat
and tap
my hair, it's own instrument in my big
sister's lap

Our great sky went from grey, to so
suddenly dark
My sister said, "pray", and so I played
my part
But my heart welled up, quicker than
rivers,
I lost my mom in a storm, and in storms
I felt with her

In an instant I opened my eyes wide and
realized,
that my mom had a song that I'd hummed
all my life
I remembered her face, and I laughed as
she sang,
"Dear island storm, please keep my boy
safe"

Adrift

It has been a few years, but I remember
it well,
the night the sky wept on her scattered
helm
The day had been kind, then a storm came
nigh,
and the crew that I knew had been thrown
from sight

The waters were dark, wind set me adrift
The revenge for parting her waters was
swift
In light of the lightening, I lowered my
eyes,
and beheld that a plank was lodged in my
side

Sure that I'd die, and with few fleeting
breaths,
I prayed, not afraid of my Heavenly rest
My blood in the dark would lure the
sharks,
A remarkable end, but a sailor's death

In the wake of exhaustion, I retired
from sight,
not a moment had passed, when I was
woken by light
What seemed like a moment had lasted
three days,
My eyes finally opened, all I saw was
her face

Her hand on my side where the plank had
            been,
  and with bandages laid over most my
            skin,
she sat by my side with a look in her
            eyes,
like it'd taken too long for my life to
            begin

In the days that followed, celebrations
            went on,
  Nights before, on the shore, I was
            almost gone
And with she who found me, a romance
            begun
My marks became scars, and the days
            became months

We ate and we sang and my dance was
            critiqued,
I worked with the men and I learned how
            to speak
I was taught by the old, and the young I
            would teach,
now I write from the place I was found,
            on the beach

And with that sweet girl who nursed me
            alive,
  with blessing bestowed, I made her my
            wife
A man I've become, and with two little
            ones,

I now have a family, and I now have a
life

So thanks for the offer, but I choose
not to return
The navy won't need me, it's a younger
man's turn
I've said my goodbyes to the helm, and
the stern
The sea's still in my reach, but that
boat has burned

'Sidon

She sits on the shore as she waits for
the news
Wearing wind in her hair and converse
shoes
She hears voice in the sea, yet knows
not whose
But it beckons her eyes in adorning
blues

Her long dark mane is thrown in folds,
as she begins to hear stories the sea
has told
She desires it's flow and its glistening
hold,
even its depths find appeal as she sits
to behold

Night's midnight light rains down from
high
She feels sand in her hands as the ocean
sighs
The pulsing sea flows increasingly nigh,
As her sire's moon starts pulling tides

She was born of the sea, and he knows
her name
She can tame any beast in the sea's
domain
'Sidon, her Father, looks up from the
depths,
at the daughter he lost, whom he wishes
to claim

She's a siren by nature, but human by
trade
And she knows that the ocean will know
her name
Stolen by Zeus, she now walks on two
legs
She's a siren at night, only human by
day

The moon is the noon for the ocean's kin
And when its rays find her eyes she can
sing again
Every night, old Poseidon returns to the
shore,
to the songs of the daughter he beckons
for

He misses her mother, from whom came her
eyes
This siren he loves was born from his
wife
In the blue of her gaze, is hidden her
name
"Dear Iris, please come home again"

Rains

It washed away the progress of the chalk
upon the street,
but fed the farmers crop, and washed the
horses feet
If it wasn't for it's pouring, we'd sink
to several pains,
but who of us imagines we can understand
the rains?

Is it her, who's open wound was washed
after it bled?
Or the trucker hitched unstuck after he
couldn't see ahead
Is it the river, who led so many
creatures back to sea,
when rain unjammed a broken damn, to set
the river free?

And us, we do the things we do, and
think we must,
but rain will not abstain to find the
great and the unjust
for rain is just a name we give to all
that comes our way,
a fire's smoke, a broken yoke, an object
of our blame

She's the mother, the one who raises
some of what we sew,
but washes all the chalk that we must
love and then let go

A merchant in her purchase, in spilling
Heaven's purse,
quite delighted in the writings and ink
of cloudy verse

Cursed of all that haven't called their
lot a gift of God,
carving out the valleys of its sediments
and sod
A nod to our perception, as it goes by
many names,
for you can choose what you will see,
long before it rains

Chapter V
Pain & Poison

Pleasure Never Find

My skin was sliced, but healed again,
my broken bones found place
I seek out life with love for Him,
no fear but for His face

My death retired soul would live,
this body ache and break
But I'll retain the faith I give,
in panting breaths I often take

I'd sooner die a martyrs death,
with this grin across my face,
than renounce the pain I daily feel,
for chasing after grace

As poison make my stomach churn,
and shoulders meet the sword,
I'd still brave the deepest burn
to journey with my Lord

For I could pain all of my days,
and pleasure never find,
and still be pleased to chase a life,
with only God in mind

No Sober Eyes

A poison found his blood,
he revealed his weakest link
His untrained peace of mind,
made naked by his drink

For drink brings equal footing,
while caught under its spell
For men become elated,
to see others sick as well

No drunk exceeds his friend
He's comparably, no worse
No person be found better,
when caught in poisoned curse

Man's character finds shelf,
and he speaks without a thought
He displays his lack of self,
and all he's gained for nought

Never Sang

They speak of this Earth and its "birth
from a bang"
How this life is a bite, from a
"singular" fang
"One cell," a bell, which nothing rang,
a gong with a song, never sang

"Hang your beliefs on a reef to the door
of my heart,
We're chaotic beings, as we've been from
the start
The cosmos, beauty, it's chance, you
see?"
But a life without purpose, believe you,
me,

it's pointless, tip less; we can't be
refined
With no end in sight, we can't be but
blind
Where we go, it shows we know less of
our hope
We're so lost, but we go with the flow
till we find,

That a death bed has found us, the end
is in sight
We'd drifted with clipped wings, to the
end of our life
We felt love, grasped it, and yet we
denied, the Almighty composer and His
hand in the skies

In the lies we digested, we rested still
restless
Content with our bent paradigm of
investment,
of time; we climbed further down into
death,
all the while we panting our held
breaths

So your science then, it's all fact
based?
Regarding, too, the missing links that
you face?
With all due respect, not to rain your
parade,
but to be an atheist requires faith

Panes

I didn't think I'd ever drink to lessen
all I carry
Or that by fate, I'd ever date a girl I
wouldn't marry
I never thought I'd ever swear or say a
word so flawed
I surely never thought I'd ever need the
grace of God

I hadn't plans to see how I'd react if
life got hard
I didn't know that as it goes, some cuts
never scar
No one told me how an angry fight could
hold a burn,
but in time, these are some things I
came to learn

And yet, they left it out, how good's
never far behind
How for every evil thing, there's two
good things to find
They never told me of the way in which
His grace is good,
when He forgives the things you didn't
think He ever would

Not that He couldn't do it, but then,
what's the need?
What good's a hospital if no one ever
seems to bleed?

49

We thought we wouldn't fall, so we never
                planned ahead,
by the time we stood we'd already been
                walking dead

So the aforementioned pain arose, and I
                was thrown
I never planned to break, much less yet
                to be the stone
I thought that men need no defense, not
                a thing at all,
but shelter means a dwelling place and
                sturdy walls

His plan was not to vanquish all of
                Heaven's rains
but to be the light that glistens
                through our window panes
So raise your hands and set perfection
                on its shelf
For God forgives the man who can't
                forgive himself

Chapter VI
Castles & Crowns

Treasure

Welcome to the forest,
where somewhere past the leaves,
nestled in the chorus,
of all that blue birds sing,

somewhere on a hilltop
in a chest upon green blades,
under where the sun drops,
in that place, a treasure laid

That treasure, something sweet,
put faith in some men's hands,
to find they dealt deceit,
in that forest covered land

As hopeful as she was,
that no men dwelt in lies,
she felt their peering lust
in what they deemed a prize

So treasure made a choice,
in great walls that rose above
and men ceased to rejoice,
in her treasure laden love

The treasure hadn't left,
she was more than walls around,
just a jewel less prone to theft
And her treasures did abound

She grew in seeking God alone,
her walls came falling down

Where treasure laid became a throne,
still safe in walls of trees around

Juxtaposition

A purple sash around my being,
a golden cuff and silver rings
Joy was sweet when I was young,
but hardship taught me everything

Leather cuffs could have been gold,
for leather warms, and silver colds
And I'm not sure who made it so,
but blind eyes have much to behold

Deaf ears hear great scales at length,
kings depend on poor men's strength
And I can't say who made this way
for crips to walk when others faint

Smiles shine when they're deserved,
wine is drunk when it is served
Excess drink does kindle rage,
as such, let joy be learned of age

Let wisdom grow for wisdom's sake
Please let us give, and let us take
Let us dream when we're asleep,
and give us work when we awake

For folly learned, and folly made,
for all facades and all parades,
where foolish go, wisdom trails
For one must die where one prevail

We tip the scale when both are seen
There's no kind where there's no mean

There's no peace where wasn't war,
and rich exists, when exists poor

King of Thieves

Dear King of thieves and heathens, so
      unjustly crucified
I've held back thanks too many days,
      this cannot make it right
I am a sinner, born and bred, You are my
      King indeed
Dear King of cons and killers, who's
      redeemed the likes of me,

You became the king, when we pressed
      down the crown of thorns
Though You alone were king before the
      moment You were born
One becomes the ruler over all who swear
      him in,
and we're the ones who claimed You ruler
      over all our many sins

Then saying, "it is finished", as your
      pardon unto God,
You rebuilt the bridge, that as sinners,
      we could not
No longer in our hands, You took upon
      Yourself,
the keys that grant us access to the
      very gates of hell

For You became the king of all the
      sinners we've begot
So over every form of evil, solely You
      could be the God
You who was perfection, took all us

thorns to die
So You alone, dear King, could set our
spirits right

So I know no words suffice, though I
haven't thanked enough
Dear King of all redeemed, I thank You
for Your love
You alone accomplished, what no other
could have done
So to You I give my thanks,

-A sinner, made a Son

A Spartan

Where I was born, the morn scattered
light into gold
Where I was raised, the days fell to
night within folds
There the wind held the sails of
fleeting ships on the sea,
and the dawn met the skin of the slave
and their free

Hunger of wolves led to cattle graze
But subsided at the walls of this golden
age
Shepherd with sheep, as people with
king,
even inmates sing songs in their iron
cage

Merchants sold incense, on flawless
thread,
as the actor found praise in the words
he said
Son made trade where his father tred,
and daughters diced fruit where their
mother led

The beggars all knew they'd be dead in
Rome
as a Spartan waged war for his love at
home
The queen tilled her hair with a golden
comb

And the priest pressed thumb to his
scroll and tome

Men chased skill as old men dreamed
Boys chased dogs for years, it seemed
Ships deemed worthy by careful plans
Lands with crops like quilted seams

Reams of parchment dressed by poet
The woman, aging, too wise to know it
This land, now gone, too long since
fooled
Now lost are the days as prince, I ruled

These Walls

Varied threats do round my throne,
I'm not known to throw my flag in
These four walls are crafted stone,
strong, alone, to bear a dragon

This here mind, a tempered shield,
sealed to varied wars that rage
And these weapons that I wield,
a fine defense against the mage

No praises of these peoples,
or lost treasures of the isles,
no star that strikes my steeples,
nor adversity or trial

I've defense against it all,
and will always see the morn
For I've grown to something tall,
but was weak when I was born

But on this day, by my city gate,
these walls fall under siege
All defenses, small and great,
made folly to this breach

If it had been a man or mass,
I'd surely sleep so deep tonight
But it was at last, a godly las,
that made it past without a fight

Chapter VII
Man & Myth

Brad T. Bird

He knew that men know food made well,
that men who bluff are men with tells
and to tell a fool won't mean he'll
        learn,
for wise men hold a wisdom earned

He knew the wild, sport and game,
    that reputation walks with name
That fame is fickle, class is friend,
    that men exude what lies within

He knew that men don't self proclaim,
    acts and words don't weigh the same
He tamed his impulse, kept at bay,
    he tried each several word he'd say

He knew that silence fathers thought,
    good men wear the watch they ought
That punctual men have grace inside,
    somewhere near where strength resides

He knew that good men answer God,
    that men don't seek approving nods
Quick to applaud a great thing seen,
    if it was truly great, indeed

He knew that knowledge isn't chief,
    that war says less of men than peace
But of all things seen, and all
        observed,
there's one thing he has yet to learn

He doesn't know the impact made,
though men don't boast foundations laid
For honor's kept when kept, a word,
I speak alone of Brad T. Bird

War

I questioned why these docile men
knew nothing of the strength within
They'd ache to fight, but nothing more,
for fear of being weak in war

These men with binders, men with pens,
men who'd never looked within,
for fear that what they'd likely see,
a warrior prince they'd never be

These men descendent of the lords
who conquered armies with their swords,
were ever taught a way to bluff,
for fear they'd never be enough

But remember truth from ageless song,
that in a war, all men belong
That this old war's not over yet,
the one we wage on sin a death

Remember, too, that men will stand,
with heart alive, and sword in hand
If men acknowledge all they know,
for battles fought and glory known

Belteshazzar

It had been many years since I walked
beside gold
When the king, who had dreams, had not
withered of old
I remember his fear when the angel
appeared,
in the midst of three children who, in
fire, stood cold

As my eyes did lie on the skies to
behold,
a longed for presence, once again, took
hold
One that was home, and one that I loved,
sent from above, to my place on the wold

In a moment, the music of the palace had
ceased,
all dancing and laughing; and the
country knew peace
He said, as before, with great power in
me,
"Once again, I'll reprove a king's
wicked disease"

Within minutes, Babylon's finest came
nigh,
and without much resistance, I left my
hillside
Once again to the palace, my way was
made clear

I'd been summoned to come in the palace
and hear

And as if in a dream from the night of
last,
I remembered the murals of the walls I
passed
I recalled all the halls and the idol
dolls,
And as before, like his father, saw the
king alas

He was pale, the resemblance of his
fallen sire
Every soul had bound his lips as the
king required
By now, God spoke through me that the
king would fall,
The very night that he beheld the
writings on the wall

Pondered

Many years before this world was at all
like today,
there walked a man, in desert sand,
along a rocky way
He puzzled over questions, no rest
within his mind,
and vowed to not relent until the
answers he did find

He asked why life was hard, and how
malice could exist
How some men dwelt in evil, yet some men
could resist
He insisted on response, yet heard no
word from God,
he bathed within the Jordan, he drank,
and nodded off

He woke to hunger pangs, and his hunger
drove his boot
He journeyed round the river till he
found a tree of fruit
"Man will do all in his strength to
guarantee his fill
and blind to what is evil, a hungered
man can kill"

With one desire met, he found a purse to
put his cash in,
to lust from dawn to dusk and quench his
amatory passion

"You now see, my son, will grants what
you want, solely,
and will remain a pain til' you desire
what is holy

Man will trust his power, and be blind
to malice made,
to do what he deem wise, despite what
price he pay
Mankind makes their choices to ensure
they may survive,
I ask that you go first to God, and
trust that He provide"

He sat with tilted head, thanking God
he'd not abstained,
had he never fallen short, no answer
he'd have gained
He pondered and he wondered, and came to
find it true,
that man will always seek what he
believe to be of value

Man, I Speak To You

Man, I speak to you, where have you put
your heart?
Ancestral actions point us to the paths
we shouldn't start
Man, I ask of you, where do you choose
to trod
There's a myriad of mediums which we use
to make false gods

The smoke in exhalation will not hold
the form you want
It may diffuse and fill the room, but
God is not so blunt
The Ghost in which you seek is not as
weak as fleeting breath
But He weeds out all addiction, even the
weed that leads to death

There's a woman He designed for you,
three dimensional and deep
She lies not behind a camera and isn't
limited 2D
There's spirit man inside you with
identity you seek
And believe you me, he won't be found in
pixels on a screen

There's a warrior bred inside you, not
to beat the ones you love,
but to defeat the flesh inside you, and
to fight for Him above
To discipline yourself, not to speak

pollutant slur
But to soldier in His battle, not at
ease or as you were

There is a chain that men are born with,
thrice their size at birth
And once become a man, they let it weigh
them down to Earth
But God designed this chain to bind the
flesh to its disdain,
and to pull our hearts to Heaven where
they 'ever will remain

Chapter VIII
Hearts & Harmonies

Different Scents

Her sweet words won't die till I do,
those deep words hurt all that I knew
I keep a verse if it keeps its worth,
the good Lord knows that she kept hers

She's a real fine wine, but not my cup
But if she called, I know I'd pick it up
She's loyal to him, that no one doubts,
but if she allowed, I'd take her out

I know that I won't get to love her,
The good Lord knows I'll find a lover
But she once said she'd fear to find,
a world in which I'd call her mine

She'd fear for my gaze lost about,
to find my raging flame go out
But if there's something she knows not,
it's that of her, I'm still in thought

That means she can't know the tug,
of our first hold in that first hug
It means that I find different air,
and different scents than in her hair

It took this long for me to know,
what I would have written long ago
I've took to cure these worded sores,
that "I'd be scared if I were yours"

Cradled

Be cradled by your ancient Semitic
mother
Be cradled by the first to raise you
Be cradled by her, unlike another
Be cradled within love true

Be cradled under nose you love
Be cradled by her fleck etched iris
Be cradled by her smile above
Be cradled of her old papyrus

Be nestled by her as her hair falls
Be nestled by her then as she sways
Be nestled by her as you glance at all
Be nestled by her always

She's the song that put you first to
sleep
The one that each one brings to mind
She's the kindest, sweet thing to keep
The wisest life in all of time

The Receipt

I drew on something yet untouched,
and feared for pressing in too much,
I held the clutch, and thought to write,
on something white, still known as such

Now before I trace my nail above her,
or did embark to mark, I hovered
no lover knows the things he'd say,
"but this day, I'll write a poem of her"

I saw the teller, to ensure I'd pay,
but wouldn't leave if I had my way
and as I returned, I felt them burn,
all those several things that I'd say

And so condensed a cloud of vapor,
my fingers met this paint less paper
Dark markings trailed behind the heat,
for when we meet, I seem to scrape her

And so I set out with my notes,
and pondered all that I'd emote
And yet to think, it wasn't ink,
but heat that kept down what I wrote

Die Trying

I lived a long time without living,
I didn't have much worth giving
If God hadn't been so forgiving,
I still wouldn't be where I am

But my God alone set me free,
He did it to say that He loves me
It's to Him I owe all I can be,
it's by Him that I'm not who I was

I will smile and won't try to hide it,
I'll laugh loud and will not be quiet
My life's new and I wanna try it,
I will become all that I can

I will live my life big or die trying,
I've spent too many good years crying
To stop serving God is like dying,
and I've already died enough

They either like me for me or they
don't,
something inside is saying they won't
But I know I'm not here on my own,
and so I will dance for joy

So I'll try it or I will die trying,
life's like a gift that I keep untying
I tasted life and I would be lying,
if I said that it didn't taste great

The Van

It sounds like the life, one of joy
within a van,
if I made you my wife, like I still
dream I can
If we lined the coast, light some fires
on a hill,
we'd hum and sing, do all the things I
think we will

I despise the scent of coffee, as do you
of smoke
But you'd drink it, and I would seldom
sit to stoke
But this earth would turn on, our sun
would set,
we'd sing to God and nod to all that
isn't yet

Pleasant mornings lead us in to knowing
love
City lights would rare compare to stars
above
Stormy winds would keep us under windy
skies,
but pretty sights are nothing like your
pretty eyes

We'd curly hair, sit and stare, snap and
dive,
if only we could buy a van, get up and
drive

Gas station vacations, each several day
new
The sweet bonfires, shires and the
scenic views

We'd talk to God more often than we
could need
There's no telling of the many books we
could read
Lord knows I would have a pen and plan
to write,
you'd have a camera in your hands, for
every sight

Vans still bring the thought of you into
my mind
The thought of you is often there, I
often find
And maybe one day, when our two roads
align,
we can reminisce while drifting off to
passing signs

With music in the dash, and my hand in
yours,
and not a bend or semblance of a worried
world,
confined to highway lines within our
very own van,
we'd drive on through the pines, all
without a plan

The Scarf

We came a ways and went across,
a border which I'd never crossed
He led my step and held my hand,
and made a home of foreign land

He took me where'd I'd never been,
I called it good, He said, "amen"
We found a shop where He had led,
He kissed my face and walked within

I heard Him laugh, I heard Him sigh,
He said, "it's her!", and came outside
Around His wrists it fell in folds,
in turquoise blue and brilliant golds

I asked its price, "too great for you",
He laughed, as His great smile grew
For me it costs, for you, it's free
for you are you when you're with me

As time went on, as time does fast,
by varied hands it had been passed
It had been hidden, had been tossed,
and I stood for what I thought was lost

I declared it bravely, and said it bold,
"My Father gave me what you hold,
in brilliant gold and turquoise blues,
my Father gave me something true"

They pawned me off some muted blue,
with gold that held no brilliant hue

So counterfeit and fake I grieved,
and threw it at that shameless thief

Then I glimpsed mine, wrapped my head,
with every gem and tasseled thread
Each one set in the Father's heart,
my Heaven crafted, blessed scarf

Chapter IX
Praise & Progeny

My Worship

So hungry he chose not to eat,
he read and closed his eyes
He fell into such inner peace,
that he began to cry

But still he asked of God,
"Please live through me today,
for you love life far more than I,
I beg you, have your way

"Love everyone I see,
in ways I never would
and smile through my face,
more often than I could

"For of fear of being cold,
I trust nothing of my own,
I wash my hands of self,
I appoint you to my throne

"But Lord, please hear me now,
I cannot relinquish praise
Lord, I give you all,
but let me keep my thanks

"Let me spectate to your greatness,
I release all within my grip
Except this one great thing,
Let me keep my worship"

His Praise

I'm keen to the heat as I walk on south,
with blood on my feet and a dried mouth
I'm keen to keep on, in blistering
sands,
for my Lord is bigger than these lands

I'm keen to keep song, as Heaven's
birds,
for his sword is sharper than dull words
I'm keen to give praise and to give
thanks,
for His abundant love in my riverbanks

I'm keen to keep joy, for I know I'm
won,
as all the good that could has been done
A son I was born, and as dead I'll be
laid,
but this grin for Him will not fade

I'm keen to dance on as my strengths
fails
I'm keen to peer on through a torn veil
I'm keen to gain life, counted as
nought,
for this Earth compares not to a good
God

For if I lose my limb, and haven't lost
Him,
and if my breaths gives way, but He
stays,

if this flesh of me is the half that's
done,
then what spirit left is called a son

So I'm keen to the heat as I walk on
south,
with blood on my feet and a dried mouth
and should all my life be scourged of
days,
then the good of my life will be His
praise

My Sons

In search of work to callous palms,
  I've set off for roads untamed
You curse a man who leaves his mom,
  but hope your sons will do the same

One day our own may fly the coup,
  when they resent a henceforth bliss
When they can live without a soup,
  or part from home without a kiss

For in such times, I've found myself,
  and I've got peace in knowing not,
which things I'm putting on the shelf,
  or trading for train tickets bought

My hands ran raw in heat and cold,
but I'm thankful for this tattered belt,
  for each several girl I didn't hold
  and work that I'll do somewhere else

And so I'll fight against their will
  to keep my feet in what I know
And on I'll journey past this hill,
  in hope my sons will hope to grow

Recalled

I found it, I recalled what I tried to
write, it's here
Let's discuss what I've had inside,
write 'til it appear
Everything we sense and see is based
upon a law,
it permeates from great to small, every
sense of awe

The nature of the good is that it rises
by its light,
the fate of all that's weighty is a
sinking into night
God cannot be burdened to sift and sort
and send,
for by logic of His laws in all, sin
cannot ascend

The kingdom of the Father is expanding
at its lines,
each of us a soldier, varied by His
great design
dark cannot attack the light, nor chaos
war on order,
as such, each of us expands a side of
kingdom border

Furthermore, God's sinless, and He is
not where sin is,
but sin and evil things are burned if
ever in His presence

so long ago, we reversed the order of
the what's right,
and sought to vanquish darkness, as if
that could bring light

But chase your God, sin will go, then
holiness you'll know
Cease to think you must be clean 'fore
lit with Heaven's glow
For sinlessness does not bring Him, its
He that brings the pure,
for He's concerned of hearts alone, of
that you can be sure

What manifests as holy, is what trickles
from the source,
it came of man when he had eyes solely
on his Lord
So let us not put hope in gifts, or
fruits that may appear,
but let us taste of Heaven's rains in
how our God is here

Some Summer Night

Oh my Lord, what friendships formed,
my heart has had its fill and more, I
won't forget a thing
It overflows and poureth out, its full
without a doubt,
Oh my Lord what friendships formed I
won't forget you now

I found sisters here, and finally tasted
longing,
never ever really felt such deep and
sweet belonging
Forged strong bonds of brotherhood,
saw the good in other's calling

Though I finally felt my desert winds,
I found they don't compare to friends
The sea can yield sweet memories,
but with treasuries it can't contend

The treasures that I came to hold,
what late night conversations told
The God above, who helped to craft,
sweet loving laughs in hearts of gold

Although I've got to go for now,
please smile, laugh, remember how,
to bless and give the Lord His praise,
He'll always raise what He's allowed

Know I can't come back for shells,
these churches, heights or steeples

the sea and wind could steal a grin,
but I'll return again for people

So, keep your journeys close to light,
keep His peace within your sight
in love, discern, let fires burn
and I'll return, some summer night

Little One

Little one, look for a treasure sought
after and lost
Venture to the land past their fire and
their frost
Go walk upon the water, go think, and
you'll obtain
After all is said and done, none will
say the things you say

My love, the words you craft are yours
and yours alone
If you choose to loose your spirit, the
Earth will be your throne
For what is loosed on Earth, is also
loosed amongst the sun,
but I think you already know this, now
don't you, little one?

I've seen the way you think, your great
mind is not a clock
It's more likened to a cosmos set before
the throne of God
So think first on your Father, who sent
first His son,
and work done by your hands will always
prosper, little one

Practice holding silence more than
learning how to speak
And let the God who woke you be the
first of which you seek
Practice recollection, fool's memories

are weak
Give Caesar what is Caesar's, and never
cease to think

Things come in their seasons, never quit
seeking your best
Don't sleep when you don't have to, for
balance is our rest
And soon enough, my love, when all is
said and done,
you'll find that hidden treasure, now
won't you, little one

Hearken

I was woken from my sleep by a light
which trembled me,
one that I recalled but that my eyes
weren't used to seeing
I was shaken at my core by one nostalgic
phrase of words,
a phrase my spirit missed but which my
ears had never heard

"Don't be afraid, but with your pen
write everything I say
The Lord of Spirits speaks unto the
people of this age
If he has ears, he shall hear the words
spoken to the sage
Hearken to His voice and put your pen
against the page

"Do you think Me caged, or am I limited
by time?
Can I fit into the space behind the
recess of your mind?
Am I the words inside a book, and in a
book am I confined?
Or are the words inside the Bible just
the signature I signed?

I am more than meets thine eyes, and I'm
not limited by day
The Word holds not My only words, I've
got much more to say
The authors of the Bible heard My Holy

Spirit's voice,
but their recordings aren't worth more
than a God who doesn't change

My love is unconditional, yet conditions
arise daily
Not even demons keep you from Me, so why
should you delay Me?
My love will not be broken from above or
down below,
but you believe redemption lies in some
words you may not know?

My son, hear my words, I'm not defined
by one impression
the universe is that, a single verse of
my expression
I am bigger than your notions, I have
more words than fit a book
And I reside inside your spirit, so it's
inside where you must look"

Something About

I can't get bored of you, my love.
Seeing as I've already lived a thousand
times,
and have still come back for more,
there must be something I have yet to
learn
or ache to learn again

Something about nights I can barely
remember as a child,
and the golden lights that made me feel
at home
Something about starlight skies,
and pretty eyes, and clouds over sand
dunes

Something about those hugs that seem to
last forever,
but that you never want to leave
Something about rushing water
over my head as I think about you

Or wind in my cloak as I roam
Or sand in my toes, or stones at my
fingertips
There's something about touching you,
I simply have not ceased to desire

There's something about the honeycomb,
and her lips, and the way you taste,
and thirst that hasn't been quenched

Something about the birds singing,
and harps playing, and children
laughing,
something about the song of your voice
throughout the world,
and I'd live again for those sounds

Something about fresh rain,
the smell of some hair,
and the scent of cold air,
I simply cannot cease to inhale

So, my precious one,

until I can taste you without eating
And see you, while asleep
Until I can feel you while I'm floating,
And hear you in the deep

Until I can smell Heaven's honey
suckles,
even when I hold my breath,
I'll keep living out this life,
I'll keep dying every death

Just to know you as I've known you,
down below as up above,
for the truth I've meant to show you,
I can't get bored of you, my love

He Hummed

God's been humming all my days
No matter what, he hummed the same
I cry to think of what defined,
the tune he's hummed all of my life

In highs and lows, he hummed along
Good or bad, He hummed His song
I sang and sinned, I slept and rode,
I wept and strode, He hummed

I wrote awhile, some heartfelt things,
for what I knew, so true to me
and while I wrote, He'd often sing
He'd close His mouth and hum

As I felt wind, fell for sands,
held water droplets in my hands,
I thought I knew who I'd become,
I listened close, He hummed

I talked to men, and they gave guide,
I'd cower back and often hide
I gained strength, broke some bones,
He still hummed His loving tone

It matters not what I have done,
the song He hums calls me a son
and though He hums what I'm to be,
His hum does not depend on me

Part 2:

Musings

The writings that follow were most often scrawled out to release concepts and ideas from my own mind, to be later reflected on or to simply relieve pressure. Many of them weren't written with the intention of being seen by others, but have since been put here in hopes that you receive something in reading them, as I most surely did in writing them.

Chapter I
Contemplations

Contemplation I

To all powers enviable of which men of
ancient ages possessed, for what purpose
and to what end did these powers serve?
Powers we believe we are hereto deprived
of? For as surely as the native
Americans used every part of the bison
in their own wisdom, the ancients, by
their wisdom, used every power, of which
they so methodically sought, to a
specific end, continually seeking such
utilization as to ensure that nothing
might be wasted.

But to what purpose were these powers
deployed, these accolades of knowledge
to which we're mostly ignorant? For
reason, or another, unavailable to us;
whether buried by sands, or burned up
after having been written down,
weathered after being chiseled in stone.
These powers were deployed, as far as we
can infer, in four manners: the first
being to heal, to enhance, to
accentuate, to prolong, and to enrich
the daily aspects of life. The second
being to study the inward laws by which
the human being should conduct itself,
to seek knowledge, and to what end all
of one's actions and thoughts should be
directed, so as to be conducive to
posterity, wisdom, clarity and
longevity. The third end lying in

matters of efficiency; whether in transportation, erection of architecture, or things of the like. Finally, the fourth evident end to which they extended their mastery was to prediction, prophecy, and calculative anticipation of what would later occur.

However fervently these great powers were sought, and even to the extent to which they functioned to their full capacity, what did it earn these men of old? For as our fathers have passed, those former, too, have passed. However long they lived, they met the same end as we have and will. And should any have succeeded in prolonging their material lives indefinitely, of what great merit would this be? For, in the first case, the universe is productive of successions and changes of a certain likeness, and to have witnessed this life for thirty years is the same to have witnessed it for a thousand years. And in the second case, should we seek to live in this encasement of a body as long as the angels are suffered to, would we not meet the same end as them, and rather quickly? This end being such that we long deeply to have our spirit taken up and returned to the fiery nature from which it came? For truly, to the same extent that our material nature is gregarious and seeks to be mingled in community, how much more powerfully does our spirit seek to be reunited with the whole from which it was derived?

I say then, be not envious of what men of after time sought through diligent study for so many years, or yet of the perplexing technologies for which they were productive. Instead, reverence the giver of such universal gifts, and neglect not His worship. For men of after time made productive use of His gifts, and were no closer to Him than we may now choose to be; this chiefly being the greatest power mankind has inherently ever possessed; to presently know their Father and divinity. Furthermore, this gift has been given, in equal ration, to all that have ever and will ever exist. As to this gift, those powers which you may presently need will be made known to you, and can be likened to constant arsenal at your disposal to combat the many ailments of life. In seeking chiefly this arsenal, however, the supplier of this gift will be made secondary in focus.

I'll speak plainly. The ascension of consciousness does not follow strides in technology; but strides in technology follow ascension in consciousness. There is little wisdom comparable to living fully in this present moment, of walking in your fulness of *being.* It is no secret that ailments should be cured,

poverty eradicated and the like: and
these advancements will come. They will
either be speedily recalled to our
collective memory, or they will be
painstakingly and slowly remembered. But
no power quite assisted the ancients in
the development of their technology as
their ability to put communion with the
Creator spirit first.

Contemplation II

I find that though you could behold a
million people, each more appealing than
the last, the most beautiful part you'll
discover in each is the Father's spirit
within them. That nothing can be argued
to be more beautiful than that which
gave each of them their life and their
uniqueness.

I have found that this spirit is the
most prevalent source of power within a
human, and that each individual has the
ability to call this spirit out of any
other individual, (this ability
attributed to the kinship this spirit
feels with itself). Furthermore, I find
that it is in our power to continually
call upon this spirit and nothing more
in all of our interactions, and that
this alone is sufficient to win over the
heart of any person. For I hope you
find, as I have time and time again,
that there is no defense against the
spirit of God, not one that subsists for
long, at least.

Furthermore, let it be known that should
one adhere to the virtue of only knowing
God in all He sees, for all of his days,
he may say in certainty, with his dying
breath, that he never once communed with

another human; but that he only talked
with God all the days of his life.

For others, God and creation alike, let
your love speak, and love will be
spoken. Let your love listen, and love
will be heard. Let your love be your
sight, and love will be seen.

Contemplation III

Child, where is your wisdom? Do you not
know that the ever flowing and
relentless energy of God is due to His
unchanging nature and consistently
spoken word? That the whole world is
sustained by his word, because resonance
is the holy result of His utterance?
Have you not heard that the staff of
Moses was blessed by a holy language to
alter nature when raised? Do you not
know that the very nature of the water,
down to the subatomic particle, was
raised up and altered by the resonance
in the intention of Christ Jesus? Do you
not know that the laws of physics in the
universe adhere to glory of God from
which they are derived? Do you not know
that God does not take shortcuts, and
that He is entirely capable of
installing tools in this universe by
which we may influence and cultivate
love in the world around us?

Contemplation IV

If it were beneficial to be a complicated man, I would, in fairness, endeavor to be one. Should it be discovered that it is more beneficial to be a simple man, trust that I would, in the same wise, endeavor to be such a man.

So far as I have been able, I have observed men in both states. As to the complicated man: I find that life is most difficult for a man with too many rules and laws in place as to how he ought to conduct himself. For such a man must momentarily lend energy to the scrutinization of himself that would be far more effective elsewhere.

As to the simple man: I find that few rules can effectively take the place of many in order to bring about proper utilization of faculties, according to the respective hierarchies of every area of a man's life. For instance: the body properly be directed by the mind, and the mind be wholly obedient to the heart, and the heart to the spirit.

The few rules, that I believe should be common to every man, are as follows:

The first, that one should see to the
strengthening of one's body, that it be
fit and ready to greet any work, and
that it be fed food conducive to
alertness and longevity.
The second, that one keep the mind
sharp; continually contemplating on such
things that not only represent the
goodness of the heart, but reinforce the
goodness of the heart, finding evidence
for goodness as a good servant.
And thirdly, that our heart ever be set
on the Creator, on love, on life, on
unity, on respect, on honesty, on
justice, and on kindness.
Fourthly and finally, that one live
presently. With their entire beingness
in the present moment. That they adore
and embrace their present circumstance
with virtue and gratitude. That they
innocently perceive all before them.

Contemplation V

Let us now speak of simple truths, that due to the frequency of the regurgitation of these truths, no further explanation is often needed; and as such, explanation is rarely supplied. By explanation, I mean diving into why these things are as they are; for we often find many surprises in the fruit of learning, whereas taking of the root would have taught us much more and far more quickly.

I speak of principles. Principles with many manifestations, and how fixed we are upon the manifestations and how the principles seem to elude us. To the degree that we must learn technique and tactic for applying a principle's several fruits, as opposed to wielding the root, itself a far more ample supply of defense or offense against the varied and diverse oppositions that life supplies. For as the former, (applying fruit,) is likened to wearing shoes for every different terrain you may encounter on your journey, that of snow and of sand, the latter, (wielding root,) could be likened to sprouting wings and flying by one accord through all of life.

The second simple truth is an extension

of the first thought. Namely: that because some concepts are so universally accepted, and therefor not often tried, their reasons for being so adequate are not investigated. For the sake of illustration, I'll present a personal example. I grew up in a Christian, God fearing home. It was no question that God was real to my family, that was abundantly evident. However, I was without a self evident reason of believing in His existence. And so, for the eighth year of my life, I pined at the basic question of His being real or not. Having realized a satisfactory answer, I continued on a path of questioning and answering that led me to a more comprehensive outlook than I could have hoped to have obtained, had I never asked that heretical and blasphemous question in the first place.

Rest assured, if the Father is real, He can take your questions. An emerald is no less an emerald if one questions its being an emerald or not. If God is real, there should be no trouble in inquiring of His reality. He'll simply be more apparent to the inquisitor than to the query-less. Furthermore, one only seeks depth of clarity on that which he inherently esteems of value. I find that most men, unless he is a sort of fake man, inquires only of that for which he cares. I'd say this is a more flattering

testament of devotion to the Lord than
blind adherence. God calls for open eye
intervention, tyrants asks for
cataracts. To conclude, I'd rather be in
the company of an inquisitive atheist
than a complacent theist.

Chapter II
Varied Musings

And Yawheh said,

"I am He that initiated the first
motion, of which all that is has come to
be. I am He that will love, far beyond
what you can comprehend or have learned.
I am He of which much has been written,
but that has never been done justice. I
am He that the earnest heart yearns for.
I am He of which the strong heart has
been made. I am He that has given of my
own nature, that you have been given the
gift to fight with me.

I am He that is zealous, jealous and
alive. I am He that holds an armory
greater than any conceived of elsewhere.
I am He who dawns a sword forged of what
cannot break. Covered in blood that
cannot run dry. Unsheathed for those who
will be won.

I am He that will win all. All that
opposes me is of a different kind than
that of which I am concerned. I am He
who knows your heart intimately, beyond
the tattered stains you believe are
bound to it. I am He who sets conviction
in your heart like the gems of heaven. I
am He who supplies the grace of power.

I am He that dawns power. Unable to be
dried up by your fires, unable to be
quenched by your rivers. Your wisdom is

my foolishness. Your heart's laugh is my
joy. I am He who is that of which you
are derived, I am He unto which you will
return.

I am He that romances. I am He that
binds your heart to the ones around. I
am He that is beyond what you imagined
your treasure would be. For I am all
that you love in this world. I am, of my
design, the eyes of the ones you love
and miss, the moments you yearn for. I
am all of this; the gifts you have known
and have not yet known. I am He that
walks with you in your step. I am He
that holds your hand. I am your anchor
and shield, I am the wind in your sails,
I am the song in your heart. All that
your spirit longs for, of virtues and
attributes, of events and occasion, of
all that will come to pass that blesses
any heart; all that has been laden in
you of goodness and greatness, I am.

How long will you question who I am? Do
I not speak loud enough? Do I leave
space in your heart of which I cannot
fill? Is your spirit foreign to its
Father? Have I not given you fear of me
to be alive? Is your very breath not a
testament of my power? Have I not
supplied you with more than enough to
know who it is you belong to?

How long will you question who I am? I
am Love. I am the beginning and the end.
I am more than your present concerns,
more long suffering than your entire
life. I Am that I Am.

I Am."

Ode to 2017

Dear 2017,

Thank you for breaking more than my bones, for scarring more than my forehead, for burning more than my hands, and for cutting more than my skin. Thank you for getting me caught in more than riptides, for work without pay, for waking me up to life. Thank you for giving me an abundant supply of discomfort, and an even greater supply of determination.

For without the excruciating pain of the fire and ice, without the uneasiness in my heart, without the pain in my hands, I wouldn't have grown. I got knocked down twice, and I stood up thrice. I held no grudge, cursed no deity, and never once said "I can't do it". I broke everything I was this year; not just the bad and the ugly, nor only the good and the great, but everything. What worked was questioned, what didn't work was scrutinized; all experience was evaluated, and I changed.

2018 will yield only what you choose to craft from the materials it presents: as terrible or as great as you allow. So, foster what you love, cut out what you loathe. Let your labels for yourself, mistakes and triumphs fall away with

last year, so as to reinvent yourself as
a Son or Daughter in every moment; ever
in His presence.

Choose thankfulness, choose to listen,
choose to question. Choose to dig and to
seek; to embrace the uncomfortable, and
to war against complacency. Pray not
that the pain be removed, but that you
learn to bear it. Remember that it is
better that a man think for a year
before he speak, than to be forever
bound to the word he hastily spoke.
Read, smile, worship, work and play. And
when all is said and done, you will more
closely resemble who you want to be.

P.S. thank you for longer hair, fuller
laughs, deepened friendships and better
food

Child of the Desert

Lord of Hosts and of power, make me as a
child of the desert. Reared by the
fervency of Your presence alone.
Accompanied at night by the galaxies You
formed, aware of Your majesty and how
all the luminaries pay You tribute.

El Shaddai, make me as a child of the
desert. Untethered to the luxury of the
world; well versed in what You say in
the sandy winds. Let my dry lips be
silent, lest I can add beauty through
life bringing and truthful words.

El Roi, make me as a child of the
desert. Joyful in knowing that all I
have is provided by Your hand. With
sharp eyes and keen ears, trained in a
variety of ways to see Your variety of
ways.

El Hashem, make me as a child of the
desert. Having the strength for what I
must lift, the wisdom for what I must
write, the skill for what I must fight,
and the joy and trust that You make me
to walk in. So much so, that the very
chaos which shakes the ground brings me
the uttermost peace, for I know my Lord
is speaking.

Precious Creator, let all my knowledge
and wisdom compounded, for however many
years I've walked this Earth, pay
tribute to You in the man I am to
become. May I remember in what I have
been reared, may I hold true to the
unshakable virtues of Your spirit, and
be unshakable in this world of ever
growing corruption.

Yahweh, may the storm bring me peace.
For men only look to You when they have
a need to; and when their provisions are
fully met, they look away from You.
Insomuch, let me always be a humbled
child of the desert, to always be within
need of Your presence, that I may never
turn my face from You. For Your face is
always on me. May my trust and
dependency always be Yours, that for
each and every thing that may ever go
wrong, I am going right by You. Therein
joyful, therein wild, therein lacking no
good thing.

I've been a child of the desert,
continue to grow me, solidify my
compounded knowledge, put it into
practice and polish it. Purge me of
compulsiveness. Train me in the final
art of thinking through my thoughts
before speaking them, train me in
humility, train me truth. As I overcome
this world, by Your hand and guidance

alone, I may then hope to one day become
the man you've destined me to be.

-A man of the desert

Prophecy

Prophecy clings to wisdom as warmth does
to the sun: for wisdom is the awareness
of the present moment, how each thing
connects to each other thing, how one
thing becomes another and into what
parts another thing will be resolved.
Prophecy is only confidence in the
effect of a cause, and one who is
prudent and has understanding will see
and speak of the effect as momentarily
as he perceives the cause; and many will
baffle at his ability to foresee, but I
tell you: a botanist can see a root and
predict a fruit, and those unacquainted
with vegetation will stand in amazement.
So the wise will see the roots of life,
and be familiar with the fruit that
shall be borne. But the foolish are
condemned to live a life of reaction, of
blindness, for they take no stock of the
present, and study not the things which
are. In the wise man's pursuit of being
aware of the present, he unwittingly and
without resistance beholds the future;
but in the fool's desperate attempt to
control the future, he neglects to know
both what will come to be, and all that
currently is.

Tantrum

For all I know is that to be legless
means I cannot walk, and I will not
complain. And that to have crushed lungs
means the cessation of my breath, but I
will not curse God. I know that for
every pursuit imaginable, there is some
thing that may be a hindrance or a
prohibitor thereof, excepting my power
to praise God and be thankful for what
is allotted unto me. This alone is
unwavering and revocable by no man or
power. And truly I tell you, that if I
do not bend to the will of what happens
without me, then what is without me will
surely bend to the will of that which is
within me. For Earth and life are a
child, acting out; I am not afflicted by
her tantrum, for I know that all she
desires is love, and so I love her. Soon
enough, her groaning ceases, and she
begins to cuddle me. For when I saw all
as holy, all as good, all as God, then
all responded in its holiness, goodness
and godliness. For God delights in the
continuation of His creation, and if I'm
to be a creative agent of His, I must
see as He sees, and love as He does

Like The Rivers

Sometimes, you ask God for guidance,
believing that He speaks differently to
you than all creation. I figured out a
long time ago that God sounds like the
rivers, He sounds like the forests and
fields and palaces in the sky at night.
He sounds like a sweet mother nursing
her young, an aroused lover, a satisfied
cat, and a hungry lion. I learned more
of God: how to gain wealth, how to be
great, how to avoid harm, how to find
peace; all when I decided to cease
trying to separate God's voice from
everything God's voice brought into
existence.

Thank You

In gratitude, I write:

Thank you to all that made me this way;
all that sculpted and propagated such
volition within me. Thank you, Father,
for my genome, predetermined aptitudes,
innate giftings and for such a wealth of
short comings. Thank you, dear
ancestors, for fighting, breathing,
praying, swearing and moving in such
wise that, by succession of events, I
could produce this piece today.
I thank you, ancient men that have long
since passed, that you led me so
vigilantly when I sought no such
leadership of the living. Thank you for
the sterling silver character you
displayed in your life. A character that
did well to rouse and shake awake such
qualities in myself. Qualities that, had
I not so studied you, might have lain
dormant unto my dying breath; never
producing the conviction one acquires in
pursuing qualities that seem to elude
him the more he attains them.

I thank you, nomadic tribes of the
desert, for awaking, within me, a desire
to find a place of solitude in the
Father. One where I could pray
unceasingly, and think on Him. I thank
you for how you etched into my heart the
beauty of family and progeny.

I thank you, giants, demons and angels
for how aware you made me that the
history and mysteries of earth and God
are long from being known in totality.
You made me aware that long before we
knew the science of form, we knew the
power of essence. That babes utter
scripture never studied, and that
knowledge isn't chief to the art of
knowing.

I thank you, myths, lore and legend.
That I was never without a creed,
without stories, without desire for my
life to be an epic tale, likened to
those I knew and recited. For without
such stories, I wouldn't have such a
deep seated peace that things work out
in the end for the pure of heart, for
the integrous, to the goodness of God.

I thank you, dear fools, who made
evident the existence of wisdom. To the
incessant, who made evident the
necessity of temperance. Thank you that
I was both, and was not suffered to
remain as such.

I thank you to the women who nurtured
me, that for such a time come as I was
handed off to men, such a boy as was
nurtured wasn't broken. Thank you,
women, for neglecting not to train my
every facet in such wise as you be

honored in what I do, despite my virile
and unbridled tendencies.

I thank you, strong men who initiated
me. Thank you to the same who challenged
me. That the qualities that were
nurtured were then put to fire and iron.
That what was inadequate was blotted
out, and what was excellent kept root
and bore fruit.

I thank you, father, that I was never
denied an opportunity to test and prove
my strength by you. That you made me
aware that a man's strength is tested in
more than his chest: but in the words he
speaks, in what makes him angry, in what
warrants his respect, in how he keeps in
word, and in his ability to never give
up in any cause worth fighting for.
Thank you for blessing me when you knew
not what I would do; for your abundant
trust in my heart and ability to be a
better man each day, and for your lack
of trust in what shouldn't be trusted in
a young man. Thank you for raising me in
full confidence that I belong more to
the progeny of Father God than of you.
That any person of any age is capable of
hearing His voice to the same degree.
I thank you, dear rains of life and
great hammer of habit, that by your
unceasing rapidity, the good within my
predisposed nature became unwaveringly
resolute. I speak of that innate nature

in me that is joyful, and needed not
remain so, yet did. Of my ability to
recall and retain, that could not have
been retained, but was. Of my quest to
alter my own perception of this place to
adhere to my inward sense of what was
good and noble, that could have been
rubbed out by the world, but thusfar,
has not been. In reference to the
latter, I'm thankful that, as I grew in
years and power, my unflinching
perception and projection of the world
as a good thing seemed to increasingly
alter its very state into such: further
validating that this world is what man
makes of it.

I'm thankful for writing, thankful for
storms, thankful for God in the hearts
of people. I'm thankful for these and
more, and I'll live as such.
Thank you

Your God

Your God judges, my God loves

Your God allows you to go to hell when
you die if you don't do it right,
My God does whatever He can to welcome
me into Heaven now

Your God only resides in the few hearts
of those who abide by a law He never
gave
My God I see in all, and I'm not mighty
enough to divide His spirit

Your God is Jesus who the Father sent
out of His love
My God is the Father who Jesus sought
and spoke about

Your God is a preconceived notion that
your every conflict must find
rectification for
Your God is a box constructed when you
were young that you try to stuff all the
majesty of existence into

Your God is someone you please
My God is someone pleased with me

The presence of your God is denied
within the kiss of an atheist, within
the embrace of the Buddhist, within the
smile of the Muslim

The presence of my God is
indistinguishable from the good, from
love, from truth and wisdom

Your God is exclusive to a few,
My God dwells in all

You read your Bible and discovered all
the ways we are separate
I read my Bible and discovered all the
ways we are One

Your God is incomplete, He sends His own
spirit to hell if the flesh it
accompanied doesn't speak a phrase
My God's spirit will return to Him,
having done its work

Christ is the way, the truth and the
life. I don't believe this means that we
have to pursue a different life and love
than the one we are, I believe it means
that any life and love we experience is
a manifestation and celebration of Him,
not separate from Him.

Christ is a heart matter, not a mind
matter. If my heart knows Him and
dictates the action of my mind, is that
not worth more than my mind knowing all
it could about Him but my heart never
being postured toward Him? Some reject
the thought of who they think He is
cognitively, but embrace Him wholly
within their heart.

The mind makes a great servant, but a
terrible master
If the mind serves Him, and not the
heart, there is dissonance. The converse
is true, as well. And so, we find that a
mind that follows the prompt of the
Heart is to be esteemed

Pain and Pleasure

One tireless night, after lying restless
in bed, antagonized by pain and
pleasure, I took the shirt off my back
and dove deep into my heart. After
swimming awhile, I found Love, and I
said, "I'm tired of pain, I'm tired of
being led by pleasure, can you take
these things from me?" Love smiled
softly and responded, "My son, though
all lives have love, not all lives have
pain, go and speak with Life, and he'll
tell you where pain and pleasure are."

And so, I swam to the island of Life; I
stepped onto the shore, and journeyed
into the jungle ahead, where I found
Life reading a letter from Love. I
inquired as to the letter, and Life
responded, "mother is checking in,
reminding me where I came from". I then
proceeded to ask where I might find pain
and pleasure, Life looked around and
said, "look around you, brother, all of
the splendor of my island is unseen by
you, shrouded by trees, to see pain and
pleasure, you must journey up the
mountain of perspective; for though all
that can perceive are alive, not all
that are alive choose to be ruled by
pain and pleasure".

And so, I journeyed up the mountain
perspective, and at the top I found two

figures pulling opposite ends of a rope, and in the middle, I saw my mind. Baffled, I inquired, "where'd you get my mind? How is that you came to posses what isn't yours, and so are fighting for control of it?" Their warring ceased and they stared at me quite baffled themselves, "well," they said in unison, "you gave us your mind. We just aren't sure who's rightfully supposed to have it".

"I'm rightfully supposed to have it!", I retorted, "and I'd like it back". Expressionless, their grip loosened and I took my mind in my hand, placing it in the bag I unwittingly handed it away in. Pain and Pleasure, left utterly speechless, said nothing as I made my way back down the mountain. Life grinned as he saw me coming, and I explained all that had just transpired. Life took up the letter he had been reading before, and read a line with a sweet humility, "My son, remember where you have come from, know it while you're here, and expect it where you're going, for though some may abide a short time in disarray, all will return to Love". He then proceeded to burn that precious letter, and with a calm serenity said in a reassuring tone, "don't worry, Mother will be sending another shortly".

Ecstatic and bewildered, I ran as fast
as feet could carry back to the shore,
and into the waters, swimming back as
far as I'd swum before, I found Love
again, she sweetly looked at me and
asked, "did you find what you were
looking for, my Son?" I smiled sweetly
back with the words,

"yes, and I'm giving it back to you"

Indivisible

We are the world to such as mites, and
we are the mites to such as this world,
this world being a mite to such as is
the universe, and God resides equally in
all.

But you're baffled and say, "can you
imagine the scale of it all? That our
sun is minuscule when set against most
stars, that it's unbearably small when
set against our galaxy, and our galaxy
is one of billions at least? Not to
mention atoms, and how abundant and
numerous they are, seemingly
irreducible? And yet to think, God sees
and is in it all!

You will remain of such wise until you
see that nought can exist outside of
God, and that to be an atom means to be
God, and to exist as a sun or galaxy
means to be God. For there is nought
outside of Him, whether a rock or you or
I or the sea. How would God not be privy
to all that is? For not only does He
reside in all, but all resides in Him.

"Are you saying God is in everything?"

In the first place, I'm saying that
matter has no desire to break away from
its creator; furthermore, it's very

132

existence would cease if it somehow succeeded.

In the second place, we aren't powerful enough to divide His indivisible spirit. Not that He is everything, rather, that nothing is without Him.

For God so gave us every gift and ability conceivable to aid in our pursuit of life and the living. Gifts and abilities our precious sister, the universe, has long since perfected.

As to the properties and abilities He did not bestow, you can be sure that among them are the abilities to purge ourself from God, to separate ourself from our Creator, and to divide His indivisible spirit.

Hey Grammy,

I don't know if you know it, but you're
one of my best friends. I never cared
too much that you're older than me, in
fact, I met a young girl recently with a
soul that was just like yours. She was
just on eight years old, and she moved a
bit quicker than you, but I know your
heart's still moving. She danced
something like the way I imagine you
want to, and she could sing like the way
I know your heart does.

My love, I don't know if you know it,
but you showed me what beauty looked
like. I've had the pleasure of seeing
more of beauty than my one life can
contain, but no one has quite reminded
me of the edge of Heaven the way you
have all my life. I know your life
wasn't always as bright a day as you may
have liked, but look at the brightness
that shines before you now.

Gorgeous, I know the words, "I love
you", weren't always the first off of
your lips many years ago, but I'm sure
you could try to count the times your
descendants have said those very words
to each other, and be occupied for the
rest of your remaining days.

Mother of my Mama, I owe my life to the
way you've cultivated your own, in every
way you did and every way you did not;
for the hearts of me and mine would not
be as they are if you had not been who
you were. Life has a funny way of
unfolding, precious woman, which brings
to mind a beautiful truth:

Some of your strongest moments went
unnoticed, some of your most vulnerable
moments brought about the Heaven we
currently see. I know you know this,
sweet angel, but the Father we're loved
by will always bring about His best, and
we're never sure just how, except that
we stay true to who we are in these
moments we now have.

And I never had to guess what your sweet
feet upon this Earthen temple would
bring my way: love, light, playfulness,
wisdom, care, compassion and connection.
Never once have I felt alone when I've
shared time with you, and I can't help
but imagine that God feels like that
when He's around you; never alone

Grammy, I don't know if you know it, but
you're one of my best friends. I never
cared too much that you're older than
me, in fact, I met a young girl recently
with a soul that was just like yours.
She was just on eight years old, and she
moved a bit quicker than you, but I know

your heart's still moving. She danced
something like the way I imagine you
want to, and she could sing like the way
I know your heart does. She was as
unscathed by life as you appear to be,
as bright as I know you are.

My Return

To be free isn't to be disconnected.
That's where I got confused. A ten year
old me fantasized about living without a
home, in a camper on the beach. I got my
wish, over ten years and six states
later, I'm homeless and happy.

Funny how it goes, though. Funny what
you think you know. I had to say bye to
my mother this morning with a twenty
second hug, when I really need at least
a minute to even feel her in my arms. I
looked in my Father's eyes this morning
as he said, "I believe in you", it's
amazing what those words did to my heart
half a decade ago. But Lord knows I
needed forty five more seconds in his
eyes before we'd really see each other.

Sometimes men live on more in the
lessons they taught than the words that
said it. More in the essence of their
wisdom than the method of their
teaching. I wish God could whisper into
the ears of my Father something like,
"your son looks into your iris every day
of his life, those green flecks are the
same ones I put in the sea, and the sky
grins at him like you do, and he never
feels far from you."

Sometimes I'm surprised by how much God
tells my mama, but still she's honored

when I say that talking to her is one of
my favorite ways to worship the Lord. If
only she knew that every time I hug
someone I hug her, and if you add up all
that time it's almost half my life. I
wouldn't be surprised if God's told her
that, but she won't hear it until He
tells her with my voice.

I'm proud of my sister, growing into
herself. She was always an angel, but
even angels are aware of what goes on.
Last time I left, she became a woman.
How much growth am I going to miss out
on? Is it worth the growth I'll
experience while away? I hope to Heaven
I'll get to hold her one day again and
it'll feel like it did when she was a
little girl.

My youngest sister riots under her
breath. Nature likes to fight back
because not long after the last you'll
hear her riot again. Maybe one day
she'll wake up and say, "you know, I
love things just the way they are."
Maybe that day she'll find that
everything is exactly as she wishes it
to be. I'll probably feel creation sigh
from six states away. Earth quakes tend
to happen when creation relaxes. Like
she's getting comfy for sleep because
some uncontent human ceased to stomp
their foot on her back. Creation will

sigh like that when my youngest sister
realizes the beauty of what is.

My brother, the one who grows a lot,
grew again. And became enamored with the
way he'd grown again. He could grow as
tall as the Tower of Babel, and still
have an inch or two to go if he ever
realized that you can't dwell on any one
thing for too long. What happens if you
don't chain down every part of a tree
but one? What happens if you allow the
lake to express itself in more ways than
one hole in the dam? Humility happens,
out pouring happens, and there's grace
and rain for each. Someone, anyone wise,
please keep asking my brother questions.

My brother, the one who makes people
laugh, I pray he laughs more. I pray
rest is found for his soul. I can't
remember a time he's slept since he was
fourteen. I pray his greatest
understanding is found firstly within
himself, and secondly without. Maybe the
next time he offers a correction, he'll
get it wrong. And an angel will pour
sweet honey into his gaping mouth that
lets loose the tears that have been
bound up by chords that are no longer
there. I imagine how many rivers will
flow clean again once he's cried, how
many wells he'll dig.

I love being without a home, but where
there's no home, there's no domain.
Before I have a woman, before I subdue
this whole Earth with mere glances, let
me learn to direct the animals, the
weather, or let me at least learn
perfect contentment with the way they
already are. I've got my own journey, my
own ways to learn love, my own
selflessness to enter. Maybe when I
learn it all, my family back home will
feel it and start hollering down the
alleys of these six states for my
return.

The End

A Note From the Author

I want to thank you for taking the time to read the contents of this compilation. The works here were written from 14 to 21 years of age, and range over a variety of topics. Musings of a Young Man is likely to be the only book I'll publish of this nature. Subsequent publishings will be either fiction, novels, or teaching based books. As such, I want to thank you again for reading my first work in the published world, and for your continued support.

Musings of a Young Man

Made in the USA
Middletown, DE
20 July 2019